T0083150

LUX PERPETUA

Peace and unity

for SATB choir and orchestra

JONATHAN WILLCOCKS

MUSIC DEPARTMENT

OXFORD
UNIVERSITY PRESS

OXFORD
UNIVERSITY PRESS

Great Clarendon Street, Oxford OX2 6DP, England
198 Madison Avenue, New York, NY10016, USA

Oxford University Press is a department of the University of Oxford.
It furthers the University's aim of excellence in research, scholarship,
and education by publishing worldwide

Oxford is a registered trade mark of Oxford University Press
in the UK and in certain other countries

© Oxford University Press 2000

Database right Oxford University Press (maker)

First published 2000

All rights reserved. No part of this publication may be reproduced,
stored in a retrieval system, or transmitted, in any form or by any means,
without the prior permission in writing of Oxford University Press,
or as expressly permitted by law. Enquiries concerning reproduction
outside the scope of the above should be sent to the Music Copyright
Department, Oxford University Press, at the address above

Permission to perform this work in public
(except in the course of divine worship) should normally be obtained
from the Performing Right Society Ltd. (PRS), 29/33 Berners Street,
London W1P 4AA, or its affiliated Societies in each country throughout
the world, unless the owner or the occupier of the premises
being used holds a licence from the Society

Permission to make a recording must be obtained in advance
from the Mechanical Copyright Protection Society Ltd. (MCPS),
Elgar House, 41 Streatham High Road, London SW16 1ER,
or its affiliated Societies in each country throughout the world

7 9 10 8 6

ISBN 978-0-19-338742-3

Printed in Great Britain on acid-free paper by
Halstan & Co. Ltd., Amersham, Bucks.

Text by Laurence Housman reprinted by permission of The Random House Group (UK).

Attack by Siegfried Sassoon reprinted by permission of George Sassoon for the United Kingdom and Commonwealth. For the United States of America copyright 1918 by E.P. Dutton, renewed © 1946 by Siegfried Sassoon, from *Collected Poems of Siegfried Sassoon*, and used by permission of Viking Penguin, a division of Penguin Putnam Inc.

Cover photograph: still from the film *The Battle of the Somme* (1916) by permission of The Trustees of the Imperial War Museum, London. Crown copyright, reproduced by permission of the Controller of Her Majesty's Stationery Office.

CONTENTS

1.	Requiem aeternam	1
2.	An army marches into war	7
3.	Light looked down	16
4.	At dawn the ridge emerges	25
5.	Lord, make me an instrument	33
6.	Et lux perpetua, luceat eis	39

ORCHESTRATION

2 flutes
oboe
2 clarinets
bassoon
2 horns
2 trumpets

2 percussion
- glockenspiel
- snare drum
- suspended cymbal
- clashed cymbals
- bass drum
- bell (G)
- triangle
- gong
- whip

timpani (3 pedal timpani)
harp
strings

Lux Perpetua was commissioned by the Hinsdale Township High School District 86, Music Director, Gary L. Wilhelm. It was first performed by the combined choirs and orchestra of Hinsdale High Schools, Chicago, on 23 March 1999, conducted by the composer.

Full score and parts are available from the publisher's Hire Library.

Duration: *c.* 30 minutes

The initial stimulus to write *Lux Perpetua* was a commission for a choral piece on the theme of 'Peace and Unity'. By coincidence, the time when I was considering the structure of the work and texts that might be included coincided with the eightieth anniversary of the November 1918 armistice and I spent a few days amongst the battlefields and endless cemeteries of the Great War in Flanders. There can surely be no more moving symbol of the destruction and futility of human conflict. Two months later, as I was nearing completion of the composition, my youngest child, Florence, was born. A new-born child - the innocence and hope of the world. And then, on the very night of the first performance of the work in March 1999, allied forces began saturation bombing of Kosovo in a conflict that was to prove yet again that in war there are rarely winners, but always many who suffer.

Jonathan Willcocks

Requiem aeternam dona eis, Domine, et lux perpetua luceat eis. From the Requiem Mass

The day will come when I will make for you a covenant with the beasts of the fields, the birds of the air, and the insects of the ground; and I will remove the bow, the sword, and war from the earth, and I will give you a life of peace. From the Oxford Book of Prayer

Kyrie eleison, Christe eleison, Kyrie eleison

An army marches into war. Jonathan Willcocks
From the darkness a conflict beckons, menacing every soul.
Officers drive men forward, the ranks respond with resolute stride and innocent pride,
the battle is joined.

As wave on wave of raw humanity, fresh to the blade,
knowing little of the menace of the whetstone.
Life's flickering spark snuffed dark,
so deadly a hand reaping the human harvest drawn to the sickle.

An army marches into war.
They hurl themselves to the perils that others have made.
Dear Lord, in your mercy, must it be so?
Sweet heav'n show us the way we may go.

Be silent and I will speak, listen to me, be silent and I will teach you wisdom. Job 33

Kyrie eleison, Christe eleison, Kyrie eleison

Light looked down and beheld Darkness
Thither will I go, said Light.
Peace looked down and beheld War,
Thither will I go, said Peace.
Love looked down and beheld Hatred,
Thither will I go, said Love.

So came Light and shone;
So came Peace and gave rest;
So came Love and brought Life.
And the Word was made Flesh and dwelt
among us.

Laurence Housman (1865-1959)

Let us be united; let us speak in harmony; common be our prayer; perfect be our unity. from Hindu scriptures

Kyrie eleison, Christe eleison, Kyrie eleison

At dawn the ridge emerges massed and dun Siegfried Sassoon (1886-1967)
In the wild purple of the glow'ring sun,
Smouldering through spouts of drifting smoke that shroud
The menacing scarred slope; and, one by one,
Tanks creep and topple forward to the wire.
The barrage roars and lifts. Then, clumsily bowed
With bombs and guns and shovels and battle-gear,
Men jostle and climb to meet the bristling fire.
Lines of grey, muttering faces, masked with fear,
They leave their trenches, going over the top,
While time ticks blank and busy on their wrists,
And hope, with furtive eyes and grappling fists,
Flounders in mud. O Jesus, make it stop.

Show us thy mercy, O Lord; and grant us thy salvation. from Psalm 85

Kyrie eleison, Christe eleison, Kyrie eleison

Lord, make me an instrument of Thy peace;
Where there is hatred, let me sow love;
Where there is injury, pardon;
Where there is discord, union;

Where there is doubt, faith;
Where there is despair, hope;
Where there is darkness, light;
Where there is sadness, joy.

St. Francis of Assisi (1182-1226)

Et lux perpetua luceat eis.

May we all be in peace, peace, and only peace; and may that peace come unto each of us Indian - The Vedas

Gather us in, Thou love that fillest all; G. D. Matheson (1842-1906)
Gather our rival faiths within thy fold.
Rend each man's temple-veil and bid it fall,
That we may know that Thou hast been of old;

Gather us in: we worship only Thee;
In varied names we stretch a common hand;
In diverse forms a common soul we see;
In many ships we seek one spirit-land;

Each sees one colour of thy rainbow-light,
Each looks upon one tint and calls it heaven;
Thou art the fullness of our partial sight;
We are not perfect till we find the seven;

As we are together, praying for Peace. Buddhist Litany for peace

Requiescant in pace. Amen.

Commissioned by Hinsdale Township High School District 86
Music Director Gary L. Wilhelm

LUX PERPETUA

1

JONATHAN WILLCOCKS

© Oxford University Press 2000

Printed in Great Britain
OXFORD UNIVERSITY PRESS, MUSIC DEPARTMENT, GREAT CLARENDON STREET, OXFORD OX2 6DP

Photocopying this copyright material is ILLEGAL.

A
17
S.
mp
et lux per-pe - tu -
A.
mp
et lux per -
T.
do-mi - - - ne.
B.
- ne,
(bell)
p
mp

22
S.
-a, lu - ce - at e - - - is.
A.
-pe - tu-a, lu-ce-at e - - is.
(bell)
p

27
S.
A.
T.
B.
mp
et
mp
et
p
The day will come,
p
The day will come,

31
lux per - pe - tu - a, lu - ce - at e - - is.
f
lux per - pe - tu - a, lu - ce - at e - - is.
f
mp
the day will come, the day will come,
mf
f
mp
the day will come, the day will come,
mf
f
cresc.
mp

B
35
f
38
S.
A.
unis.
mp
The day will come when I will make for you a
T.
B.
unis.
mp
The day will come when I will make for you a co - ve - nant, for you a
41
mf
co-ve-nant with the beasts of the fields, the birds of the air, and the in - sects of the
mf
mf

44
ground; and I will re-move the bow, the sword, and war from the earth, and I will
f
ff
mf
47
give you, and I will give you a life of peace, a life of
and I will give you, will give a life of peace,
mf
C
50
peace, of peace.
p
(bell)

55
S.
A.
S.A. semi-chorus
p
Ky - - ri - e e - lei - - - - son.
60
p
Chri - - - - - - - ste e - lei - son.
(bell)
64
p
Ky - - ri - e e - le - - -
67
son.
dying away
pp

2

71
Threatening ♩. = 92
Orch. red.
p
mp
mp
cresc.
D
75
S. A.
T. B.
unis. mf
sim.
An ar - my
mf
cresc.
ff
mp
79
unis. mf
sim.
An ar - my mar - ches, an ar - my mar - - ches,
mar - ches, An ar - my mar - ches, mar - ches in - to
mf

82
mar - ches in - to war.
war.
mf
An
mf
84
mf cresc.
An ar - - my mar -ches, mar - ches in - - to war.
mf cresc.
ar - my mar -ches, mar - ches in - to war.
f
From the
E
86
f
From the dark - ness a con - flict bec - - kons,
dark - ness a con -flict bec - - kons, me - na -cing ev-ery soul.
From the
f
f

88
from the dark - ness bec - kons,
Of - fi -cers
dark - ness a con - flict...
Of - fi -cers
90
mf cresc.
drive men for - ward; the ranks res - pond, with re - so -lute
drive men for - ward;
mf cresc.
with re - so -lute stride,
sim.
92
stride, and in - no - cent pride, the bat - tle is joined.
and in - no - cent pride, the bat - tle is joined.

F
94
the bat - tle is joined.
As wave on
97
wave of raw hu - - ma - ni - ty,
fresh to the
99
blade, know - ing lit - tle of the me - - - - nace of the
cresc.

101
whet - stone. Life's flick - er - ing spark snuffed dark, so
103 unis.
dead - ly a hand rea - ping, rea - ping, rea - ping
unis.
105
the hu - man har - vest drawn to the sic-kle.

G
108
mf
An ar - my mar - ches, an
An ar - my mar - ches, an ar - my
mf
111
ar - my mar - - - ches, mar - - ches in - to war.
mar - ches, mar - ches in - to war.
113
mf cresc.
They hurl them - selves to the
mf cresc.
They hurl them - selves to the per - ils that oth - ers have

H
115
per - ils that oth - ers have made.
Dear Lord, in your mer - cy,
made.
mf
mf
mp
118
must it be so?
Sweet heav'n, sweet heav'n,
mp
mp
mp
122
sweet heav'n, show us the way we may go.
p
p
p

** (or semichorus). Solo voices should be, if possible, from within the choir.*

137
rall.
a little slower
S.A semi-chorus
p
S.
A.
Ky - - ri - e e - lei - - - son.
will teach you wis - dom.
wis - dom, will teach you wis - dom.
rall.
a little slower
(bell)
p
142
p
S.
A.
Chri - - - - - ste e - lei - son,
Ky - ri -
147
e e - lei - - - - son.
dying away
pp

3

Peacefully ♩ = 72
152
S.
A.
T.
B.
p
Light looked down
p Light looked
Peacefully ♩ = 72
mp
157
mf
and be - held dark - ness,
down
p
Light looked down
and be - held dark - ness,
Light looked down
p
p
Light looked down
and be - held dark - ness,
p Light looked down
p
Light looked down and be - held dark - ness,
mp

163
p
Thi - ther will I,
p
Thi - ther will I go,
p Thi-ther will I go,
p Thi - ther will I go,
J
167
p
mf
thi -ther will I go, said Light.
p
Peace looked down
mf
thi -ther will I go, said Light.
p Peace looked down
p
Peace looked down
mf
thi -ther will I go, said Light.
Peace looked
p
p
mf
thi -ther will I go, said Light.
mp

172
f
and be - held war,
f
and be - held war,
down
p
Peace looked down and be - held war,
f
p Peace looked down
p
Peace looked down and be - held war,
f
177
mf Thi - ther will I
mf Thi - ther will I go

K
180
mp
Thi-ther will I go, said peace.
p
Love looked down
mp
Thi-ther will I, thi-ther will I go, said peace.
p Love looked
mp
Thi-ther will I go,
mp
thi-ther will I go, said peace.
go,
mp
thi-ther will I go, said peace.
mp
185
and be - held
down
p
Love looked down
and be - held
p
Love looked down
p
Love looked down
and be - held
p
Love looked down
p
Love looked down and be - held

190
ff
ha - - tred,
unis. mp
Thi - ther will I go,
ff
ha - - tred.
unis. mp
Thi - ther will I go,
ff
ha - - tred,
unis. mf
Thi - ther will I go,
ff
ha - - tred,
unis. mf
Thi - ther will I go,
ff
mp
L
194
mp
thi - ther will I go, said Love.
So came Light and shone;
mp
thi - ther will I go, said Love.
So came Light and shone;
mp
thi - ther will I go, said Love.
So came Light and shone;
mp
thi - ther will I go, said Love.
So came Light and shone;
mp

200
mp
So_ came Peace and gave rest;
mp
So_ came Peace_ and gave rest;
mp cresc.
So_ came
mp
So_ came Peace and gave rest;
mp
So_ came Peace and gave rest;
mp cresc.
So_ came Love,
mp
cresc.

205
mp cresc.
So_ came Love,
mf cresc.
and brought_ Life;
and_ the
Love,
mf cresc.
and brought_ Life;
and_ the Word,
mp cresc.
So_ came Love,
mf cresc.
and brought_ Life;
and_ the
mf cresc.
and brought_ Life;
and_ the Word,
mf

208
mp
Word was made Flesh, and dwelt
mp and dwelt
and the Word was made Flesh,
and dwelt
mp and dwelt
Word was made Flesh,
and dwelt
mp and dwelt
and the Word was made Flesh,
mp and

M
213
a - mong us.
a - mong us.
a - mong us.
dwelt a - mong us.
gently
p

218
ALTO SOLO
mp
Let us be un - i - ted, let us speak in har - mo -
BASS SOLO
mp
Let us be un - i - ted, let us speak in har - mo - ny;
222
- ny; com - mon be our prayer; per - fect be our
com - mon be our prayer;
cresc.
226
rall.
un - i - ty, per - fect be our un - i - ty, per - fect be our
per - fect be our un - i - ty, per - fect be our
rall.

S.A. semi-chorus
a little slower
230
p
Ky - - ri - e e - lei - - son.
Chri-
un - i - ty.
un - i - ty.
a little slower
(bell)
235
S.
A.
- - - - - - ste e - lei - son.
Ky - ri -
239
e e - le - - - son.
dying away
pp

4

Slowly ♩ = c.72
244
S.
A.
T.
B.
Slowly ♩ = c.72
p
p
250
p
At dawn the ridge e - - mer - ges massed and
p
p
p
254
dun in the wild pur - ple of the glow - 'ring sun,

258
mp
Smoul - der - ing through spouts of drift - - - ing smoke that
mp
Smoul - der - ing through spouts of drift - - - ing
mp
Smoul - der - ing through spouts of drift - - - ing smoke that
mp
Smoul - der - ing through spouts of drift - - - ing
260
3
shroud the me - na - cing scarred slope;
smoke that shrouds the me - na - cing scarred slope;
shroud the me - na - cing scarred slope;
smoke that shrouds the me - na - cing scarred slope;

N
263
mp
27
and
mp
unis.
and one by one tanks creep and
with heavy tread
mp
sim.
268
unis.
one by one tanks creep and top-ple for- ward to the wire.
top-ple for- ward to the wire.
O
a little faster
272
mf cresc.
mf
3
The bar - rage roars and lifts. Then, clum- si - ly
mf cresc.
The bar - rage roars and lifts.
a little faster
mf

275
bowed with bombs and guns and sho - vels and bat - tle - gear,
mf
Then, clum - si - ly bowed with bombs and guns and sho - vels and
f
sim.
278
poco a poco accel.
mf
men jos - tle and climb to meet the brist - ling
bat - tle - gear,
mf
poco a poco accel.
sim.
sim.
281
mf
fire.
Lines of grey, mut tering fa - ces, masked with fear,
mf
sim.
sim.

285
poco a poco accel.
f
3
while time ticks
they leave their tren - ches, go-ing ov - er the top,
poco a poco accel.
sim.
sim.
289
blank and bu - sy on their wrists,
f
sempre poco a poco accel.
and hope, with fur - tive eyes
f
sempre poco a poco accel.
sim.
sim.
292
and grap - pling fists,
f
floun - ders in mud.
f
floun - ders in mud.
sim.
sim.

P
broadly ♩ = c. 82
295
ff
O Jes - us, make it stop, O Jes - us,
O Jes - us, make it stop, O
O Jes - us, make it stop, O Jes - us,
broadly ♩ = c. 82 O Jes - us, make it stop, O
298
f
poco a poco rall.
mf dim.
make it stop, make it stop, make it stop,
Jes - us, make it stop, make it stop, make it stop,
make it stop, make it stop, make it stop,
Jes - us, make it stop, make it stop, make it stop,
poco a poco rall.
mp

303
SOPRANO SOLO
mp gently
mf
Show us thy mer - cy, show us thy mer-cy, O Lord;
TENOR SOLO
mf gently
Show us thy mer-cy, O Lord;
S.
p
mp
make it stop. O Lord, make it
A.
p
mp
make it stop, O Lord, make it
T.
p
mp
make it stop, O Lord, make it
B.
p
mp
make it stop, O Lord, make it
309
mp
and grant us thy sal - va - tion, and grant us thy sal-va - tion.
mp
and grant us thy sal-va - tion, and grant us thy sal - va - tion.
dim.
p
stop. Sal - va - tion,
dim.
p
stop. Sal - va - tion,
dim.
p
stop. Sal - va - tion,
dim.
p
stop. Sal - va - tion,

314
S.A. semichorus
mp
Ky - - ri - e e - lei - - son, Chri - - -
S.
p
sal - va - tion
A.
p
sal - va - tion,
T.
p
sal - va - tion,
B.
p
sal - va - tion,
(bell)
p
(bell)
p
319
- ste e - lei - son. Ky - ri - e e - le - - - son.
p
rall.
pp
sal - - va - tion
pp
sal - - va - tion.
pp
sal - - va - tion.
pp
sal - - va - tion.
(bell)
p
rall.
(bell)
pp

5

For Florence, newly born, the innocence and hope of the world

338
un - ion,
where there is doubt,
faith.
Q
341
p cresc.
S.
Lord, make me an in - stru - ment,
Lord, make me an in - stru - ment,
A.
p cresc.
mf
Lord, make me an in - stru - ment,
Lord, make me an
p cresc.
345
mf
Lord, make me an in - stru - ment of Thy peace,
Thy
in - stru - ment of Thy peace,
of Thy peace,
Thy
mf
349
S.
A.
p
peace.
p

R
353
S.
A.
T.
B.
p
Lord, make me an in - stru - ment of Thy peace;
p cresc.
unis.
where there is des-
p
357
mp cresc.
where there is dark ness, light,
-pair, let there be hope,
mp cresc.
cresc.
361
where there is sad - ness,
where there is sad - ness,
p

365
mp cresc.
may there be joy,
mf cresc.
may there be joy,
mp cresc.
may there be joy,
mf cresc.
may there be
cresc.
mf cresc.
369
f cresc.
ff
mf
may there be joy!
joy!
joy, may there be joy!
joy!
f cresc.
ff
f
mp
S
374
p cresc.
S.
Lord, make me an in - - stru - ment,
Lord, make me an
A.
Lord, make me an in - - stru - ment,
T.
O
B.
O Lord,
p cresc.

377
in - - stru - ment, Lord, make me an in - stru - ment of Thy
Lord, make me an in stru - ment of Thy peace, of Thy
Lord, Lord, make me an in - stru - ment of Thy
O Lord, make me an in - stru - ment of Thy
380
ALTO SOLO
mp
May we all be in peace,
BASS SOLO
mp
May we all be in
S.
A.
T.
B.
peace, Thy
p
peace,
peace, Thy peace,
peace, Thy peace,
p
p

384
mp
peace, and on - ly peace, and may that peace come un-to each
mp
peace, peace, and on - ly peace, and may that peace come un-to each
peace, peace, Thy peace,
389
p
of us.
p
of us.
p
Thy peace.
p
p
392
rall.
pp

6
395
Solemnly
♩=c. 66
S.
A.
mp
et
Solemnly
♩=c. 66
(bell)
p
401
lux per-pe - tu - a, lu - ce - at e - - is.
lux per - pe - tu-a, lu-ce-at e - is.
T
406
S.
A.
T.
B.
mp cresc.
3
(bell)
Ga - ther us in,
p

411
mf cresc.
Ga-ther us in, thou love that fill-est
mf cresc.
Ga-ther us in, ga-ther us in,
mp cresc.
Ga-ther us in,
mf cresc.
ga-ther us in, thou love that fill-est
ga-ther us in,
mf cresc.
ga-ther us in, ga-ther us in, thou love fill'st
cresc.

414
f
all, ga-ther our ri-val faiths with-in thy
ga-ther our ri-val faiths,
ga-ther our ri-val faiths with-in thy
all, ga-ther our ri-val faiths with-in thy
all, ga-ther our ri-val faiths, ga-ther our faiths with-in thy

416
f
fold.
Rend each man's tem-ple- veil and bid it fall,
fold.
Rend each man's tem-ple- veil and bid it fall,
fold.
Rend each man's tem-ple- veil and bid it fall,
fold.
Rend each man's tem-ple- veil and bid it fall,

419
mf
that we may know that thou hast been of old.
mp
Ga-ther us
that thou, hast been of old.
Ga-ther us in,
that we may know that thou hast been of old.
Ga-ther us in,
may know that thou, hast been of old.
Ga-ther us in,

U
422
mf
in, gather us in.
ga - ther us, ga - ther us in.
ga - ther us, ga - - - ther us in.
ga - ther us in.
427
mp
S.
A.
SOLI
T.
B.
As we are to - ge - - ther,
pray - ing for peace
pray - ing for
pray - ing for peace
pray - ing for
Ga - ther us in;
Ga - ther us in;
Ga - ther us in;
Ga - ther us in;

430
SOLI
peace.
peace.
mp
— we wor - ship on - - - ly thee; in va - - ried names we stretch a com - mon
mp
— we wor - ship thee; in va - - ried names we stretch a com - mon
mp
— we wor - ship on - - - ly thee; in va - - ried names we stretch a com - mon
mp
— we wor - ship thee; in va - - ried names we stretch a com - mon

mf
433
Let us be tru - ly with each o - - ther.
SOLI
Let us be tru - ly with each o - - ther.
Let us be tru - ly with each o - - ther.
mf
Let us be tru - ly with each o - - ther.
mp
hand; In di - verse forms
mp
hand; In di - verse forms
mp
hand; In di - verse forms
mp
hand; In di - verse forms

436
SOLI
mf
3
pray - ing for peace,
pray - ing for
mp
— a com - mon soul we see;
in ma - ny ships we seek one spi - rit - land;
— a com - mon soul we see;
we seek, one spi - rit - land;
— a com - mon soul we see;
in ma - ny ships we seek one spi - rit - land;
— a com - mon soul we see;
in ships we seek, one spi - rit - land;

V
439
SOLI
peace.
mp cresc.
Ga - ther us in,
ga -ther us in.
Ga - ther us in,
ga - ther us, ga - ther us in.
Ga - ther us in,
ga - ther us ga - - - ther us in.
Gather us in
ga-ther us in.
cresc.
(bell)
mp

442
445
mf cresc.
f
mf cresc.
S.
A.
Each sees one co-lour of thy rain - bow - light,
each looks up-on one tint and calls it
T.
B.
mf cresc.
f
mf cresc.
mf
mf
448
f
f
heaven;
Thou art the full - ness of our par - - tial sight;
f
f
mf

451
mf
we are not per - fect till we find the seven;
mf
453
S.
mp
Ga - ther us in.
A.
mp
Ga - ther us in, ga - ther us, ga - - - ther us in,
T.
mp
Ga - ther us in, ga - ther us in.
B.
mp
Ga - ther us in, ga - ther us in,
mp

455
mf
ga - ther us in.
ga - ther us in, ga - ther us, ga - - - ther us in,
ga - ther us in, ga - ther us in.
ga - ther us in, ga - ther us in.
W
457
f
mf
S.
A.
SOLI
As we are to - geth - er, as we are to - geth - er,
T.
B.
mp
p
pray - - ing for peace, pray - - ing for

461
SOLI
mp
peace,
p
peace,
mp
p
p
peace,
peace,
pp
peace.
p
pp
(bell)
p
X
466
SEMICHORUS
S.
A.
mp
Re - - qui - es - cant in pa - - ce.
mp
Re -
S.
p
A - - men.
A.
p
A - - men.
T.
p
A - - men.
B.
p
A - - men.
p
(bell)
p

472
S.
Semi
A.
p
– qui - es - cant in pa - - ce,
pa - - - ce,
A - - - men.
A - - - men.
A - - - men.
A - - - men.
(bell)
pp
477
rall.
pa - - ce.
A - - - men
A - - - - - men.
(bell)
rall.